LET'S GET STARTED!

SIGHT READING & RHYTHM EVERY DAY®

Helen Marlais, Kevin Olson, and Julia Olson

DAY ONE 1   DAY TWO 2   DAY THREE 3   DAY FOUR 4   DAY FIVE 5

★ L E S S O N   D A Y

T H E
F·J·H
M U S I C
COMPANY
I N C.
Frank J. Hackinson

Production: Frank J. Hackinson
Production Coordinators: Peggy Gallagher and Philip Groeber
Cover: Terpstra Design and Andi Whitmer
Cover and Interior Illustrations: Nina Crittenden
Text Design and Layout: Terpstra Design, Maritza Cosano Gomez, and Andi Whitmer
Engraving: Tempo Music Press, Inc.
Printer: Tempo Music Press, Inc.

ISBN-13: 978-1-61928-035-9

ABOUT THE AUTHORS

Dr. Marlais is one of the most prolific authors in the field of educational piano books and an exclusive writer for The FJH Music Company Inc. The critically acclaimed and award-winning piano series, *Succeeding at the Piano® A Method for Everyone, Succeeding with the Masters®, The Festival Collection®, In Recital®, Sight Reading and Rhythm Every Day®, Write, Play, and Hear Your Theory Every Day®,* and *The FJH Contemporary Keyboard Editions,* among others, included in *The FJH Pianist's Curriculum®* by Helen Marlais, are designed to guide students from the beginner through advanced levels. Dr. Marlais has given pedagogical workshops in virtually every state in the country and is an FJH showcase presenter at the national piano teachers' conventions. As well as being the Director of Keyboard Publications for The FJH Music Company, Dr. Marlais is also an Associate Professor of Music at Grand Valley State University in Grand Rapids, Michigan, where she teaches piano majors, directs the piano pedagogy program, and coordinates the young beginner piano program. She also maintains an active piano studio of beginner through high school age award-winning students.

Dr. Marlais has performed and presented throughout the U.S., Canada, South Korea, Italy, England, France, Hungary, Turkey, Germany, Lithuania, Estonia, China, Australia, New Zealand, and Russia. She has recorded on Gasparo, Centaur and Audite record labels with her husband, concert clarinetist Arthur Campbell. Their recording, *Music for Clarinet and Piano,* was nominated for the 2013 *International Classical Music Awards,* one of the most prestigious distinctions available to classical musicians today. She has also recorded numerous educational piano CD's for Stargrass Records®. She has performed with members of the Chicago, Pittsburgh, Minnesota, Grand Rapids, Des Moines, Cedar Rapids, and Beijing National Symphony Orchestras, and has premiered many new works by contemporary composers from the United States, Canada, and Europe. Dr. Marlais received her DM in piano performance and pedagogy from Northwestern University, her MFA in piano performance from Carnegie Mellon University, and was awarded the Outstanding Alumna in the Arts from the University of Toledo, where she received her bachelor of music degree. Visit: www.helenmarlais.com

Kevin Olson is an active pianist, composer, and member of the piano faculty at Utah State University, where he teaches piano literature, pedagogy, and accompanying courses. In addition to his collegiate teaching responsibilities, Kevin directs the Utah State Youth Conservatory, which provides weekly group and private piano instruction to more than 200 pre-college community students. The National Association of Schools of Music has recently recognized the Conservatory as a model for pre-college piano instruction programs. Before teaching at Utah State, he was on the faculty at Elmhurst College near Chicago and Humboldt State University in northern California.

A native of Utah, Kevin began composing at age five. When he was twelve, his composition, *An American Trainride,* received the Overall First Prize at the 1983 National PTA Convention at Albuquerque, New Mexico. Since then he has been a Composer in Residence at the National Conference on Keyboard Pedagogy, and has written music commissioned and performed by groups such as the American Piano Quartet, Chicago a cappella, the Rich Matteson Jazz Festival, MTNA (Music Teachers National Association), and several piano teacher associations around the country.

Kevin maintains a large piano studio, teaching students of a variety of ages and abilities. Many of the needs of his own piano students have inspired more than 100 books and solos published by The FJH Music Company Inc., which he joined as a writer in 1994.

Julia Olson got her start teaching piano in Utah where she also taught preschool at a private school that emphasized learning through music. Since then, she has taught private piano lessons as well as early childhood music and group piano classes in California and Illinois. She is a member of the National Music Teachers Association and the Early Childhood Music and Movement Association. In addition to maintaining a piano studio with children of all ages, Julia has been the director of several church children's choirs and is the director of a children's choir in her community.

HOW THE SERIES IS ORGANIZED

All rhythmic activities

All sight-reading activities

Place a ✔ when you have been successful!

Each unit of the series is divided into five separate days of enjoyable rhythmic and sight-reading activities. Students complete these short activities "Every Day" at home, by themselves. Every Day the words, "Did It!" are found in boxes for the student to check once they have completed the rhythm and sight-reading activities.

The new concepts are identified under each unit title. Once introduced, these concepts are continually reinforced through subsequent units.

On the lesson day, there are short rhythmic and sight-reading activities that will take only minutes for the teacher and student to do together.

TIPS FOR STUDENTS

★ For the rhythm exercises, always count aloud with energy in your voice and with confidence!

★ For all the Sight Reading exercises, play with a big, warm tone. Remember to play to the bottom of the keys to produce a beautiful sound.

★ You can play the Sight Reading exercises detached (with space in between the notes), or smoothly *(legato)*. Some exercises have these *staccato* and *legato* marks already for you. Your teacher will help guide you.

Have fun playing "Let's Get Started!"

FJH2171

TABLE OF CONTENTS

Unit 1 - Fun in the Sun

Guide Note Middle C with 2nds and 3rds

Rhythm—Clap and count aloud. Whisper the rests. Then speak the words in rhythm while you point to each note or rest.

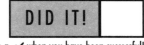

Place a ✔ when you have been successful!

1.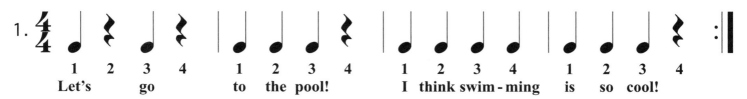

   1   2   3   4   1   2   3   4   1   2   3   4   1   2   3   4

Let's   go   to the pool!   I think swim - ming is so cool!

2.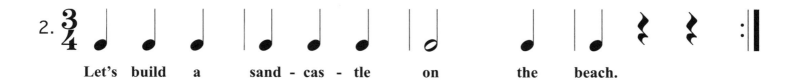

Let's build   a   sand - cas - tle   on   the   beach.

Sight reading—Clap and count until the rhythm is easy. Then plan the 2nds silently on the top of the keys.

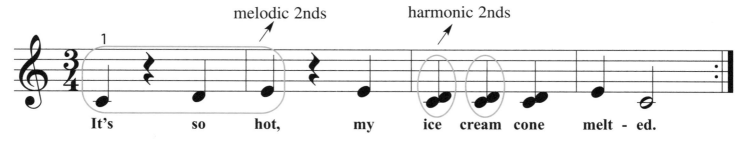

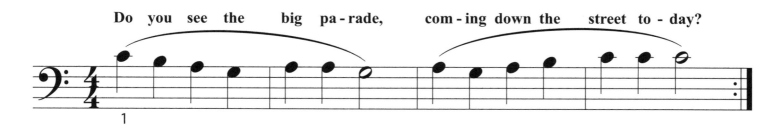

Rhythm—Clap and count aloud. Whisper the notes. Then speak the words in rhythm while you point to each note or rest.

DID IT!

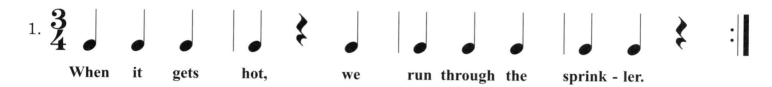

1. When it gets hot, we run through the sprink - ler.

2. My old dog gets la - zy in the sum - mer - time.

 Sight reading—Point to each note and rest as you count aloud. Play the harmonic 2nd before you begin.

DID IT!

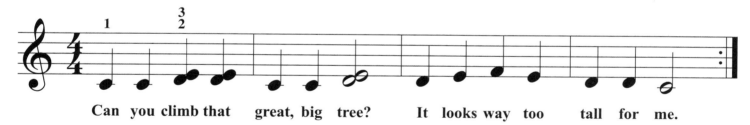

Can you climb that great, big tree? It looks way too tall for me.

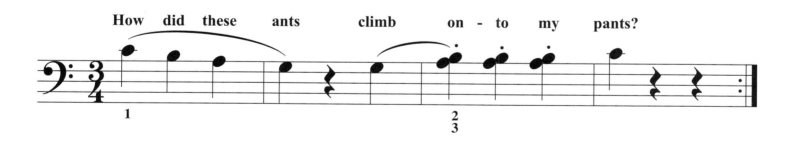

How did these ants climb on - to my pants?

Rhythm—Point to each note or rest as you count aloud. Keep it steady.

DID IT!

1. I get to go on a fam - 'ly va - ca - tion.

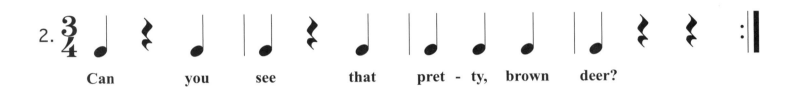

2. Can you see that pret - ty, brown deer?

Sight reading—Find and play the harmonic 2nds and then the harmonic 3rds, naming them aloud as you play.

DID IT!

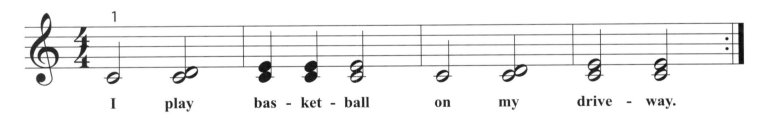

I play bas - ket - ball on my drive - way.

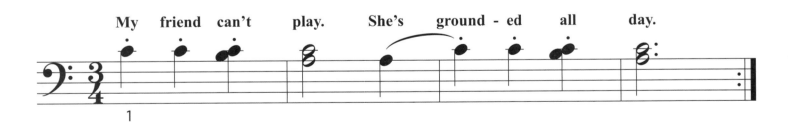

My friend can't play. She's ground - ed all day.

FJH2171

Rhythm—Tap the rhythm on your thighs while counting aloud.

DID IT!

1.
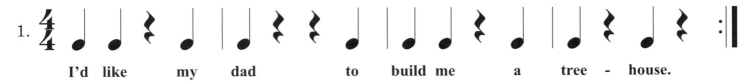

I'd like   my   dad   to   build me   a   tree - house.

2.

It would be   so   cool   to   go   to   sum - mer   school.

 Sight reading—Circle the harmonic 3rds. The first one has been done for you.

DID IT!

I   like   to   hang   up - side - down   on   the   mon - key   bars.

Bees,   bees,   bees!   There are   bees up   in those   trees!

Rhythm—Close the fallboard of the piano and tap and count aloud with energy.

 DID IT!

1.

My friend Ei - leen broke her leg on her tram - po - line.

2.

It's hot to - day. Let's find some shade.

 Sight reading—Plan the direction of the notes. Plan the repeated notes in each example. Play only when you think you can play from beginning to end without stopping.

DID IT!

Let's sell lem - on - ade out in front of my house.

I hear the ice cream truck! Quick, go get some mon - ey!

 Rhythm—Clap and count aloud. Then speak the words in rhythm while you point to each note or rest.

DID IT!

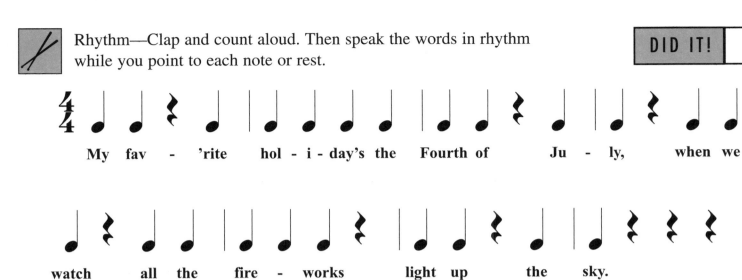

My fav - 'rite hol - i - day's the Fourth of Ju - ly, when we

watch all the fire - works light up the sky.

ENSEMBLE PIECE Duet—Count aloud as you play.

Fishing with Dad

Student part

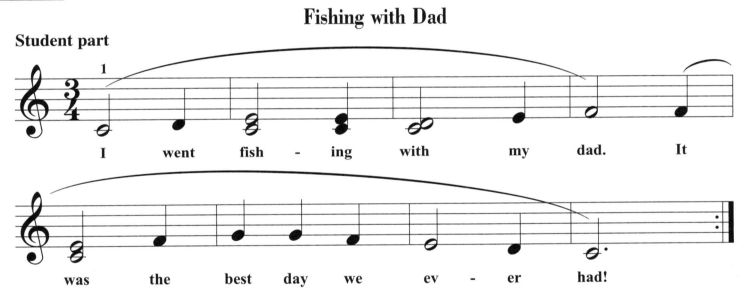

I went fish - ing with my dad. It

was the best day we ev - er had!

Teacher accompaniment (student plays as written)

L.H. legato

? After playing, ask yourself, "Did I keep my eyes on the music and not my hands?"

Unit 2 - At the Farm

Guide Note Treble C with 2nds and 3rds

Rhythm—Tap with your right hand and count aloud. Whisper the rests.

DID IT!

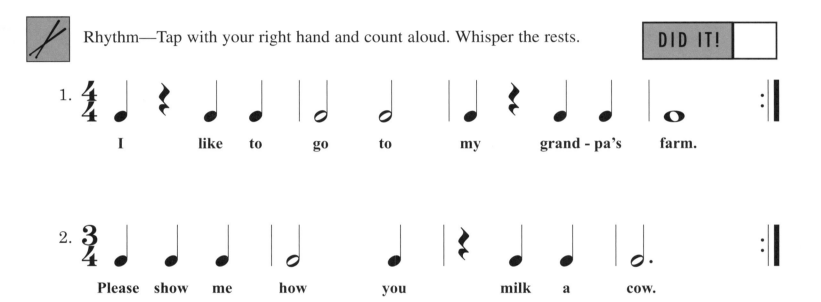

1. I like to go to my grand - pa's farm.

2. Please show me how you milk a cow.

Sight reading—Circle the Guide Note Treble C's. Notice this note is the **3rd space** in the treble clef. Be sure to relax your wrist while playing.

DID IT!

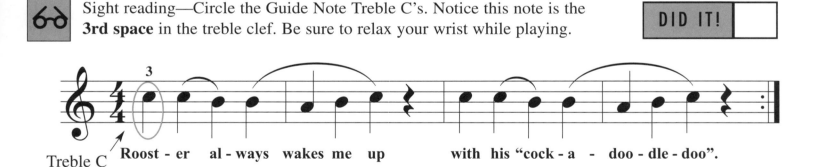

Treble C

Roost - er al - ways wakes me up with his "cock - a - doo - dle - doo".

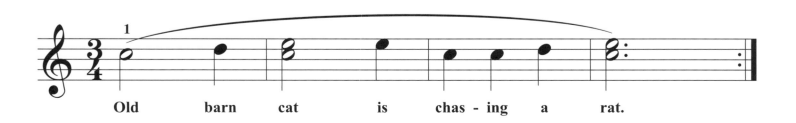

Old barn cat is chas - ing a rat.

Rhythm—Clap and count with energy! Move your arms out to the side for every quarter rest.

DID IT!

1. Let's pick   some   ap - ples   and   make a home - made   ap - ple pie.

2. Ba - by   pig was   born to - day.   I   want   to   name him   Jay.

 Sight reading—Play these exercises silently on the top of the keys. Then play with confidence.

DID IT!

Gal - lop - ing,   gal - lop - ing,   my   horse   is   gal - lop - ing.

Ev - 'ry   morn - ing   we   have to gath - er   eggs.

Rhythm—Tap the rhythm with both hands on your thighs.

DID IT! ☐

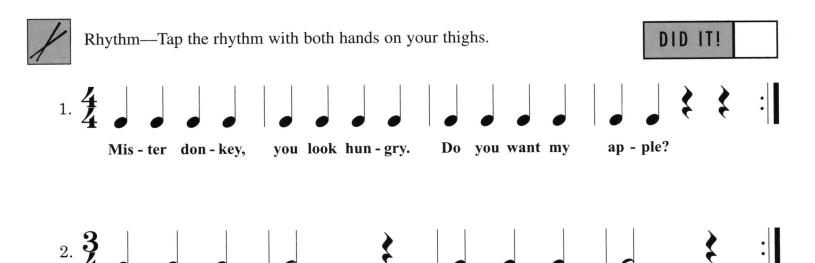

1. Mis - ter don - key, you look hun - gry. Do you want my ap - ple?

2. Ducks in the pond swim all day long.

 Sight reading—Notice the 2nds and 3rds and the repeated notes.
Counting aloud *while you play* will help you keep a steady beat.

DID IT! ☐

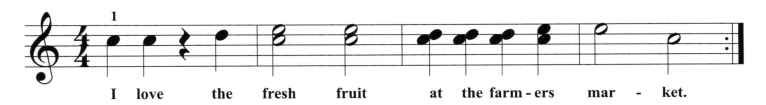

I love the fresh fruit at the farm - ers mar - ket.

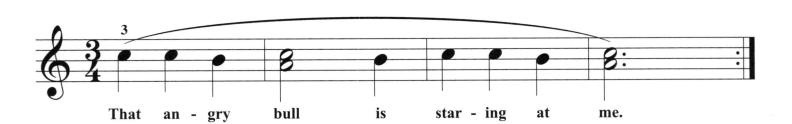

That an - gry bull is star - ing at me.

DAY FOUR

 Rhythm—Tap the first example with your right hand. Tap the second example with your left hand.

DID IT!

I think my coat got eat - en by a goat.

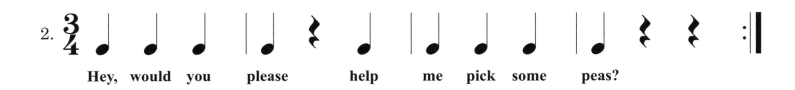

Hey, would you please help me pick some peas?

 Sight reading—Circle the melodic 3rds. Plan the repeated notes.

DID IT!

Great, big tire—— swing on my grand - pa's ma - ple tree.

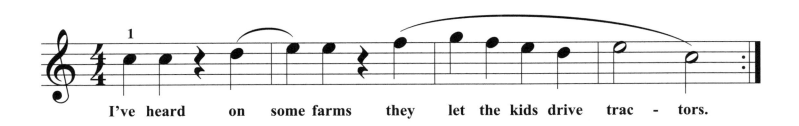

I've heard on some farms they let the kids drive trac - tors.

Rhythm—Clap and count aloud with confidence! Then speak the words in rhythm while you point to each note or rest.

DID IT!

1.

In the sum - mer the corn grows o - ver six feet tall.

2.

Let's have a square dance out by the barn.

  Sight reading—Plan the direction of the notes. Play only when you think you can play from beginning to end without stopping.

DID IT!

I need some boots 'cause the farm is ver - y mud - dy.

Ti - ny chicks go "cheep, cheep, cheep cheep."

 Rhythm—Listen to your teacher speak the words while you point to each note. Then speak the words too!

DID IT!

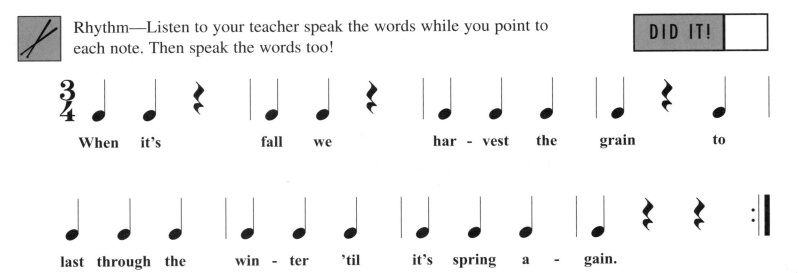

When it's   fall we   har - vest the   grain   to

last through the   win - ter 'til   it's spring a - gain.

Duet—Silently play on the top of the white keys. Notice the harmonic 3rds.

Farm Dog

Student part

Farm dog's   so   la - zy, he   does - n't   chase   sheep,   he

is - n't   a   watch - dog,   he   just likes   to   sleep.

Teacher accompaniment (student plays as written)

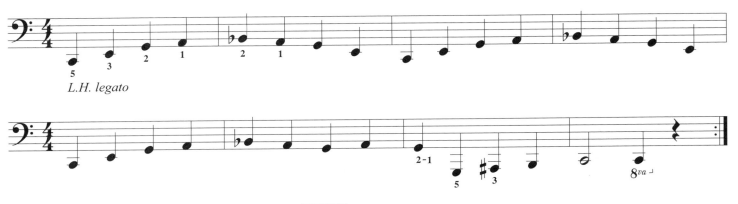

L.H. legato

? After playing, ask yourself, "Did I play with a steady rhythm?"

Unit 3 - Weather Watching

Guide Note Bass C with 2nds and 3rds

Rhythm—Write in the time signatures. Then, clap and count.
Finally, speak the words in rhythm.

DID IT!

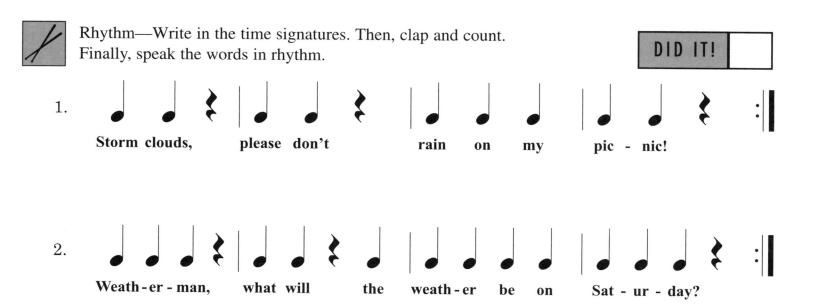

1. Storm clouds,   please don't   rain   on   my   pic - nic!

2. Weath-er-man,   what will   the   weath-er   be   on   Sat - ur - day?

Sight reading—Circle all the Guide Note Bass C's. Notice this note is the
3rd space down in the bass clef. Be sure to relax your wrist while playing.

DID IT!

I   hope   it   starts to rain to   make the   grass   green a - gain.

Bass C

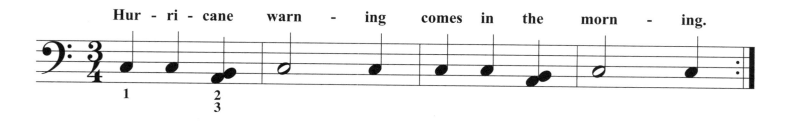

Hur - ri - cane   warn - ing   comes   in   the   morn - ing.

FJH2171

Rhythm—Feel the steady beat as you clap and count aloud. Then clap and speak the words.

DID IT! ☐

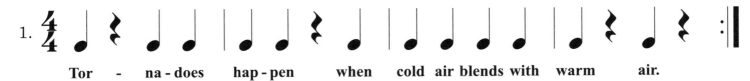

1.

Tor - na - does hap - pen when cold air blends with warm air.

2.

It's hot to - day, I'll find some shade.

 Sight reading—Circle the Guide Note Bass C's. Keep your eyes on the music as you play.

DID IT! ☐

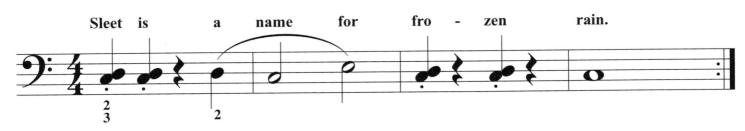

Sleet is a name for fro - zen rain.

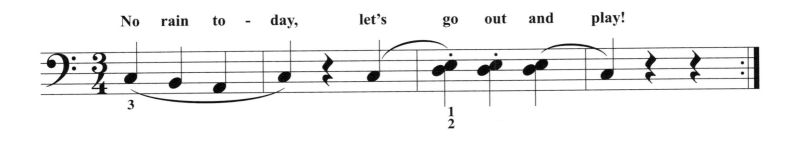

No rain to - day, let's go out and play!

Rhythm—Tap and count one example medium loud (*mf*); then medium soft (*mp*).

1. Too much wind to - day, it blew my hat a - way.

2. Where did I put my um - brel - la?

 Sight reading—Plan the harmonic 3rds. Remember to play with a flexible wrist.

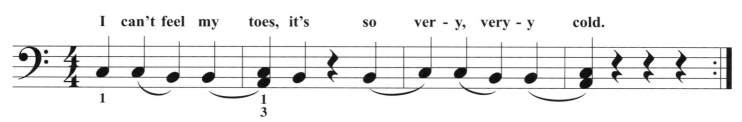

I can't feel my toes, it's so ver - y, very - y cold.

Part - ly cloud - y, part - ly sun - ny, what is the dif - f'rence?

Rhythm—Speak the words with confidence. The rests (silences) are just as important as the notes.

DID IT!

1.

I - ci - cles   are   a   tas - ty   treat.

2.

I   think the   best thing on   a   sun - ny day   is   lem - on - ade.

 Sight reading—Keep your eyes on the music and count as you play. Play at a "thinking" tempo so you never stop.

DID IT!

Right   be - fore   dawn,   there's   frost   on   the   lawn.

My   cous - in   Joe   has   nev - er   seen   snow.

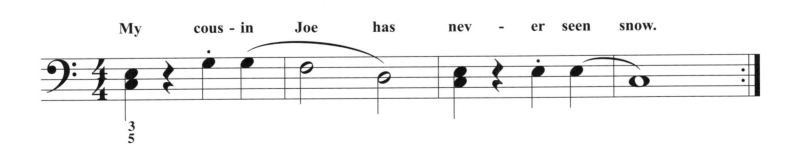

Rhythm—Tap the first example with your right hand. Tap the second example with your left hand.

 DID IT!

1.

Do   your   hear   a   breeze   blow - ing   through   those   ap - ple   trees?

2.

Cu - mu - lus   clouds   are   white   and   puf - fy.

 Sight reading—Slowly and silently play these melodies on the top of the keys. Then play both examples, moving your arm along with each finger.

DID IT!

Pit - ter,   pat - ter,   pit - ter,   pat - ter,   rain - drops   on   my   win - dow   pane.

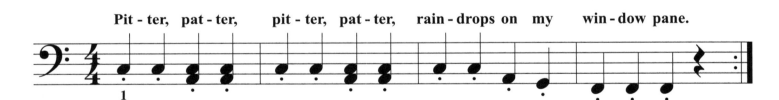

1

Fog   is   just   a   cloud   on   the   ground.

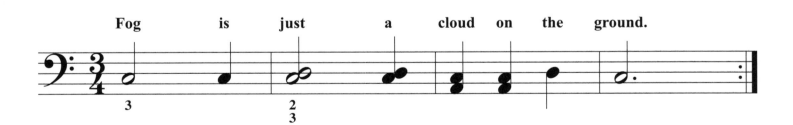

3   2
                 3

 Rhythm—Write in the time signature. Then tap and count aloud.
Finally, speak the words in rhythm.

DID IT!

What   a   per-fect day!   Sev'n-ty-five de - grees and sun.

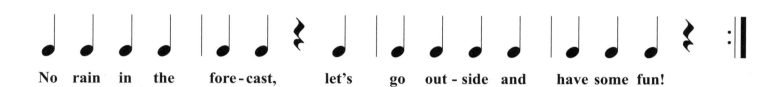

No   rain   in   the   fore-cast,   let's   go   out-side and   have some fun!

 Duet—Plan the piece by playing it *slowly* on your thigh. Move your arm directly behind
each finger that plays.

Snow Day

Student part

It   snowed   all   night,   and   that's   real - ly   cool.   To -

day   is   a   snow   day,   they've   can - celled   our   school!

Teacher accompaniment (student plays as written)

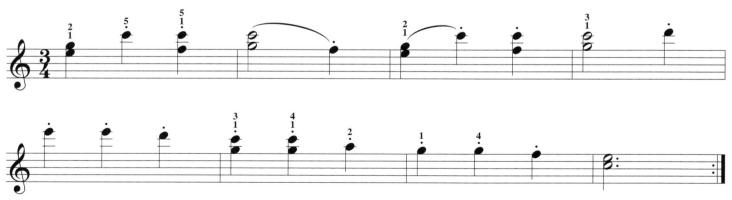

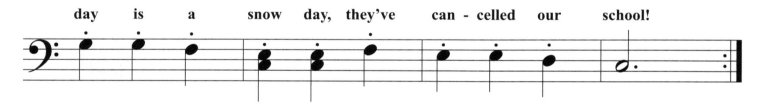 After playing, ask yourself, "Did I play with a
steady beat without stopping?"

Unit 4 - Camping Trip

Guide Note Treble C with 2nds, 3rds, 4ths, and 5ths

 Rhythm—Set a strong pulse and tap without stopping. Then speak the words in rhythm.

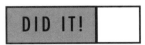 **DID IT!**

1.
Roast - ing marsh - mal - lows by the camp - fire.

2.
Did you bring your com - pass? I think that we are lost.

 Sight reading—Circle the intervals of a 4th before playing. The first one has been done for you.

DID IT!

I think that's a bear, it's stand - ing o - ver there.

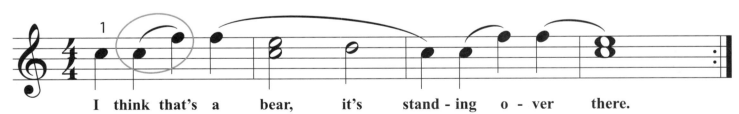
I need some bug spray for all these mos - qui - toes.

Rhythm—Let your arms swing as you count, and then speak the words.   DID IT! ☐

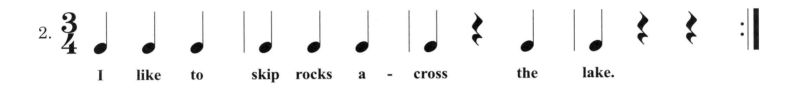

1. Far   from the   cit - y   the   stars   look so   pret - ty.

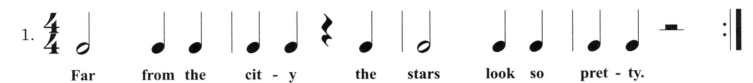

2. I   like   to   skip rocks   a - cross   the   lake.

 Sight reading—Circle the Guide Note Treble C's. The first one has been done for you. Then plan the intervals.   DID IT! ☐

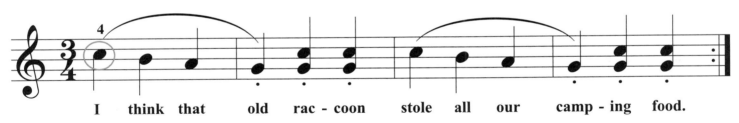

I   think that   old   rac - coon   stole all   our   camp - ing   food.

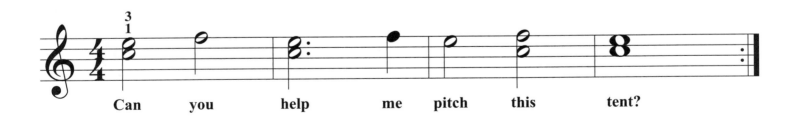

Can   you   help   me   pitch   this   tent?

Rhythm—Sway your body from left to right as you keep a steady beat. DID IT!

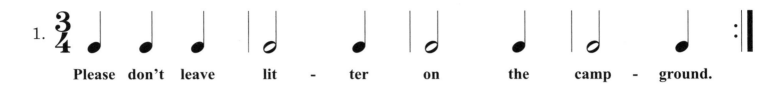

1. Please don't leave lit - ter on the camp - ground.

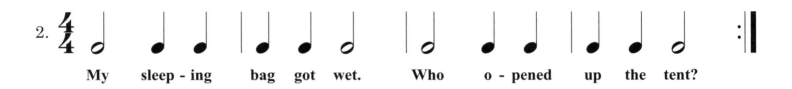

2. My sleep - ing bag got wet. Who o - pened up the tent?

 Sight reading—Say the name of each interval as well as the direction aloud as you play. For example: 4th down, 4th up, 2nd down, etc. DID IT!

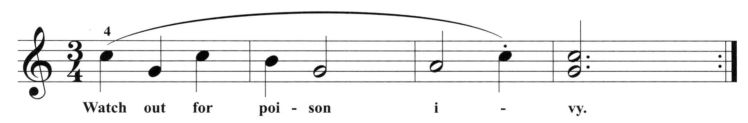

Watch out for poi - son i - vy.

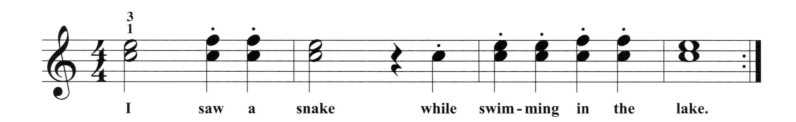

I saw a snake while swim - ming in the lake.

FJH2171

Rhythm—Point to the notes as you speak the words in rhythm.

DID IT!

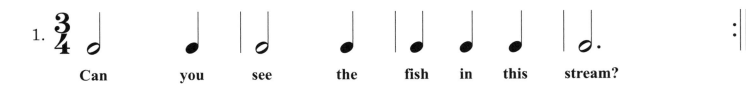

1.

Can you see the fish in this stream?

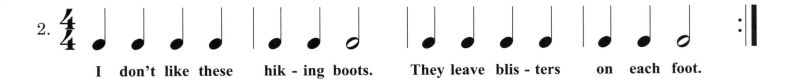

2.

I don't like these hik - ing boots. They leave blis - ters on each foot.

 Sight reading—Always look ahead to the next measure when playing and not at your hands. Remember where the Guide Note Treble C's are.

DID IT!

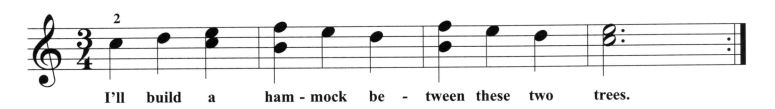

I'll build a ham - mock be - tween these two trees.

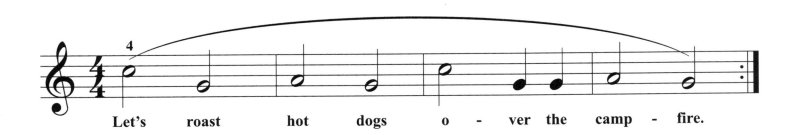

Let's roast hot dogs o - ver the camp - fire.

Rhythm—Close the fallboard and tap on it. Count aloud with energy!

DID IT!

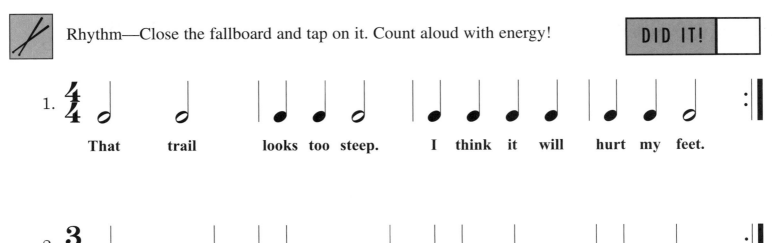

1. That trail looks too steep. I think it will hurt my feet.

2. I can hear coy - o - tes howl - ing.

Sight reading—Plan the intervals. Play only when you think you can play from beginning to end without stopping.

DID IT!

Bring your har - mon - i - ca or your gui - tar.

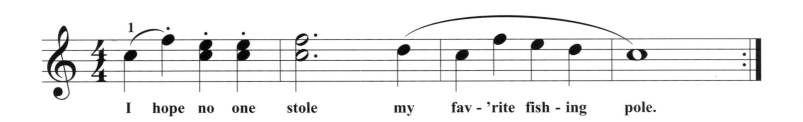

I hope no one stole my fav - 'rite fish - ing pole.

 Rhythm—Clap the rhythm with your teacher. Then speak the words in rhythm.

DID IT!

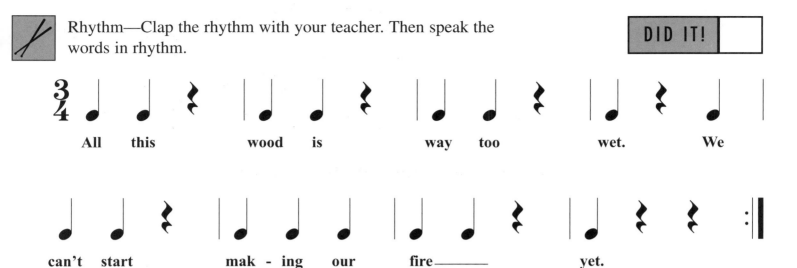

All this wood is way too wet. We can't start mak - ing our fire—— yet.

Duet—Your teacher will give you 45 seconds to silently play this piece on the top of the keys.

Big Hike

Student part

Why are you sleep - ing so late to - day? We've got a big hike planned, so don't de - lay!

Teacher accompaniment (student plays as written)

? After playing, ask yourself, "Did I play without stopping?" If so, great!

Unit 5 - Under the Sea

Guide Note Bass C with 2nds, 3rds, and 4ths

 Rhythm—Speak the words in rhythm while you point to each note or rest. **DID IT!**

1. Sci - en - tists   still find   new   spe - cies   of   fish.

2. O - ceans   cov - er   more   than   half   the   earth.

 Sight reading—Circle the Guide Note Bass C's. The first one has been done for you. Plan the intervals before starting to play. **DID IT!**

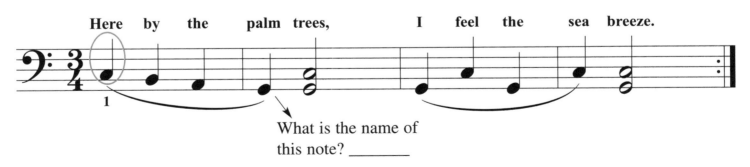

Here by the palm trees, I feel the sea breeze.

What is the name of this note? _____

Blue whales are the larg - est crea - tures in the world.

FJH2171

Rhythm—Tap the first example with your right hand. Tap the second example with your left hand.

1.

I've   nev - er swam with sharks.   I   hope   I   nev - er will!

2.

I   like sea - food,   all types of   sea - food.

 Sight reading—Play without stopping, always counting aloud. Go slowly enough so you play all the notes correctly.

She   sells   sea - shells   by   the   sea - shore.

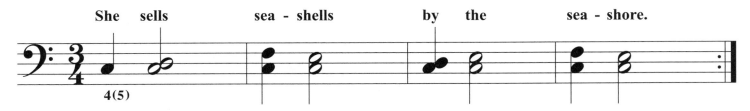

4(5)

Great   big   oc - to - pus,   I hope you don't   fol - low us!

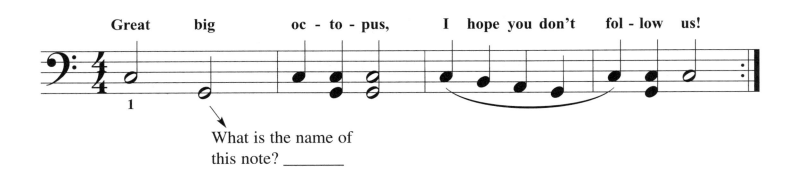

1

What is the name of
this note? _____

Rhythm—Count as steadily as a clock ticks! Then speak the words in rhythm.   DID IT!

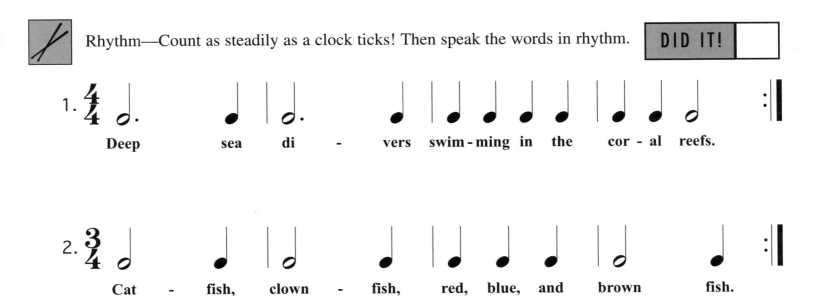

1.
Deep   sea   di - vers swim - ming in the   cor - al reefs.

2.
Cat - fish,   clown - fish,   red, blue, and   brown   fish.

Sight reading—Find and circle the 4ths. Then plan the 2nds and 3rds and begin!   DID IT!

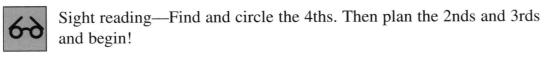

If there's   a   jel - ly fish, how 'bout a pea - nut   but - ter fish?

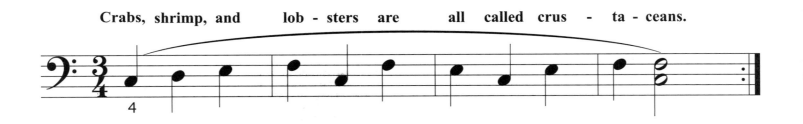

Crabs, shrimp, and   lob - sters   are   all called crus - ta - ceans.

Rhythm—Tap with both hands, keeping a steady beat.

1.

Star - fish　　　float　so　　grace - ful - ly.

2.

Sea cows,　　or　man - a - tees eat　plants and　al - gae　in　the　sea.

 Sight reading—Before playing, say aloud where the 2nds and 4ths are. Play the examples slowly, always looking ahead to the next measure.

Down in　　our　sub - ma - rine,　we ex - plore the　　o - cean floor.

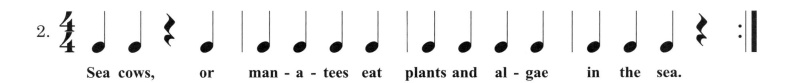

1

Dol - phins　are　play - ing,　wa - ter they're spray - ing.

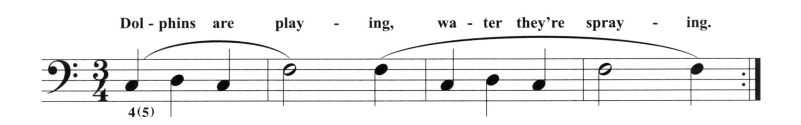

4(5)

Rhythm—Clap and count with confidence! Then speak the words in rhythm while tapping. 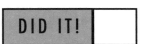 DID IT!

1.

Sea   a -   nem - o - ne   look like plants un - der the sea.

2.

I   like   to   go down - town   to   the   a - quar - i - um.

 Sight reading—Keep your eyes on the music and count as you play. Play at a "thinking" tempo so you never stop. 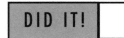 DID IT!

Pi - ra - nha,   pi - ran - nha   are fish with   sharp teeth.

Fish   that   glow   use   bi - o - lu - mi - nes - cence.

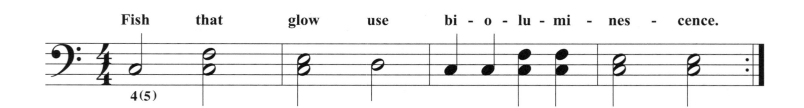

Rhythm—Speak the words in rhythm confidently for your teacher. **DID IT!**

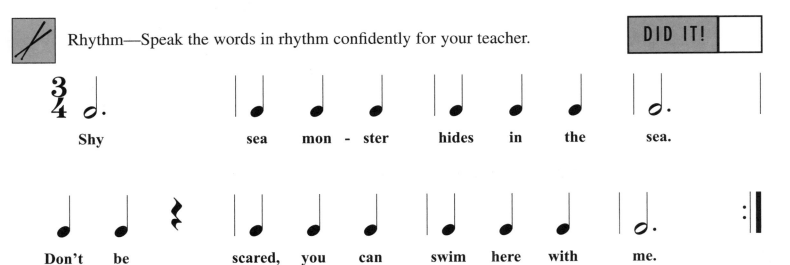

Shy — sea mon - ster hides in the sea.

Don't be scared, you can swim here with me.

 Duet—Play slowly and evenly with your teacher. Listen for the two-note slurs while you play.

Dolphins

Student part

Dol - phins look like they have smiles.

They can swim for miles and miles.

Teacher accompaniment (student plays as written)

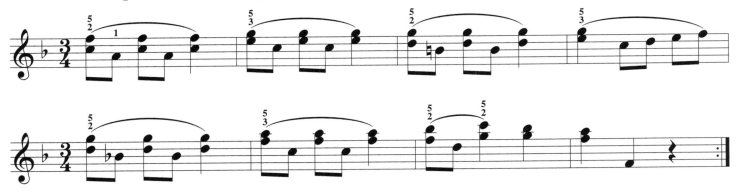

? After playing, ask yourself, "Did I play the notes correctly?" If so, terrific!

Unit 6 - Feathered Friends

Guide Note Treble C with 2nds, 3rds, 4ths, and 5ths

Rhythm—Choose Bass C or Treble C position and make a melody from these examples.

 DID IT!

1.

Os - trich - es   lay   the   world's big - gest   eggs.

2.

Some   birds   mi - grate o - ver   ten   thou - sand   miles!

Sight reading—Circle all the Guide Note Treble C's and the High G's. The first ones have been done for you.

 DID IT!

My friend's par - a - keet can talk.   It can al - so squeak and squawk.

Fun - ny fla - min - go,   where did your   leg   go?

FJH2171

Rhythm—Tap the first example loudly (strongly) ($\boldsymbol{f}$) and the second example quietly ($\boldsymbol{p}$).

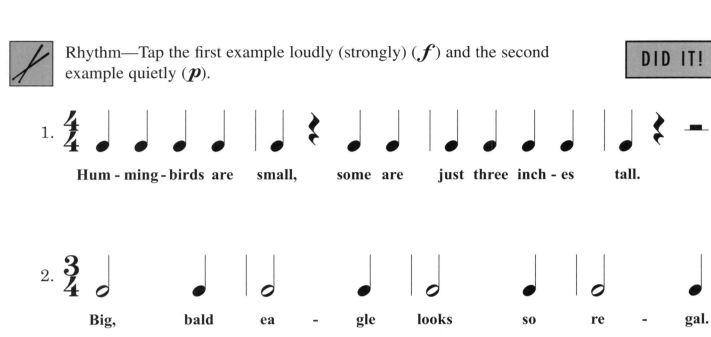

1. Hum - ming - birds are small, some are just three inch - es tall.

2. Big, bald ea - gle looks so re - gal.

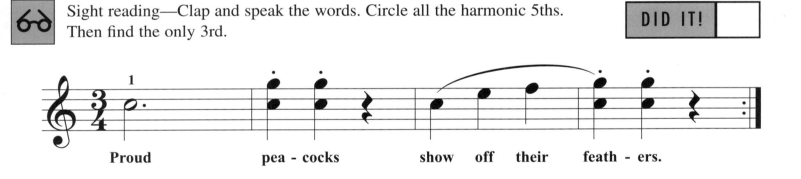

Sight reading—Clap and speak the words. Circle all the harmonic 5ths. Then find the only 3rd.

Proud pea - cocks show off their feath - ers.

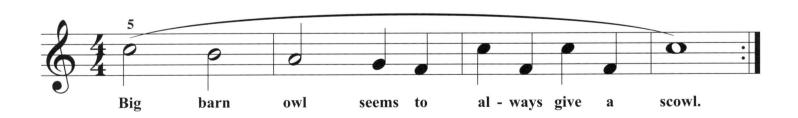

Big barn owl seems to al - ways give a scowl.

Rhythm—Tap the first example with your right hand. Tap the second example with your left hand. 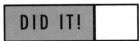 DID IT!

1.

Tou - cans   have ver - y   col - or - ful   bills.

2.

I wish I could fly   like birds up in the sky.

 Sight reading—Play slowly so that you will play correctly and evenly. DID IT!

Wood - pec - ker, stop peck - ing, I can - not sleep!

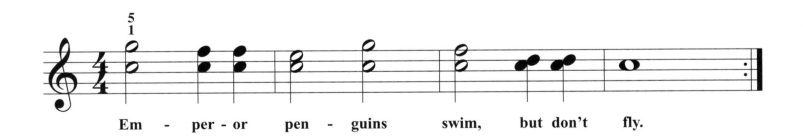

Em - per - or pen - guins swim, but don't fly.

Rhythm—Tap steadily on your thighs as you speak the words in rhythm.

DID IT!

1.

Ev - 'ry   fall,   I   see   geese   fly - ing   south.

2.

Moth - er duck   leads her lit - tle duck - lings 'cross the   road.

Sight reading—Keep your eyes on the music as you play and don't stop.

DID IT!

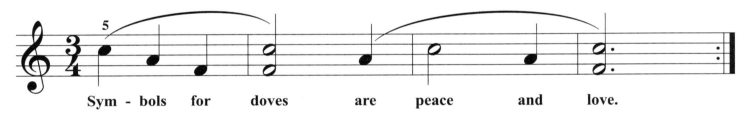

Sym - bols   for   doves   are   peace   and   love.

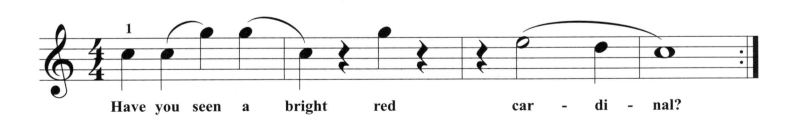

Have you seen a bright red   car - di - nal?

Rhythm—Speak the words in rhythm, accenting the downbeats. **DID IT!** ☐

1.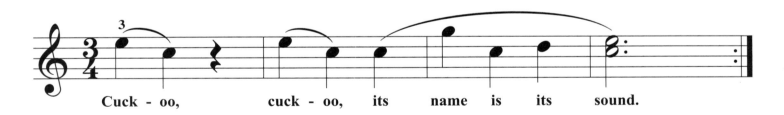

Sci - en - tists that stu - dy birds are or - ni - thol - o - gists.

2.

Hawks and fal - cons are birds of prey.

 Sight reading—This time, say the letter name of the notes as you play.
Then, listen as you play without saying anything. **DID IT!** ☐

Cuck - oo, cuck - oo, its name is its sound.

I see a loon ev' - ry af - ter - noon.

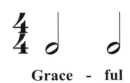 Rhythm—Say the words in rhythm—first slowly, then the second time, quickly.

Grace - ful swan swims in the lake at dawn.

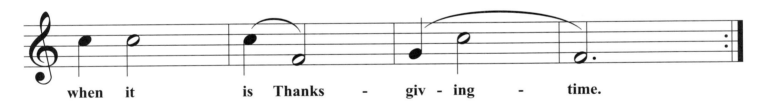

He takes flight a - bove the lake at night.

 Duet—Say the intervals for your teacher. Then play while counting. Let your arm move along with each finger that plays so that your wrist is flexible.

Old Tom Turkey

Student part

Old tom tur - key likes to hide

when it is Thanks - giv - ing - time.

Teacher accompaniment (student plays as written)

L.H. legato

 After playing, ask yourself, "Did I look at the music and not my hands?" If so, great!

Unit 7 - Circus Time

Guide Note Bass C with 2nds, 3rds, 4ths, and 5ths, Guide Note Low F

Rhythm—Set a steady pulse and speak the words.

DID IT!

1.

| Can | you | | find | where | they | sell | cot - | ton | can - | dy? |

2.

| Sad | cir - cus | clown, | turn your | frown | up - side | down. |

Sight reading—Circle all the Guide Note Low F's. The first one has been done for you. Then play, enjoying the intervals of a 5th.

DID IT!

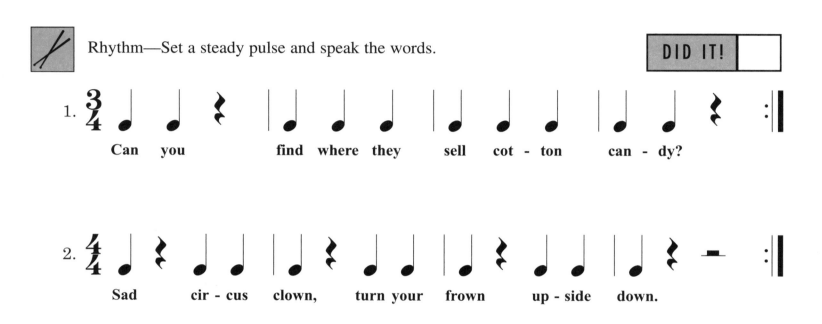

Big, brown bear rides a bike o - ver there.

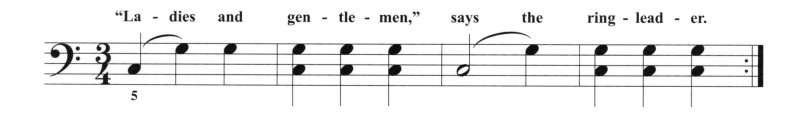

"La - dies and gen - tle - men," says the ring - lead - er.

Rhythm—Say the words in rhythm while pointing to each note.

1.

An - cient Ro - mans in - ven - ted the cir - cus.

2.

Girls on the high tra - peze, fly - ing a - round with ease.

 Sight reading—Circle the intervals of a 5th (one has been done for you). Then plan the rest of the intervals before you play.

Did you know an - oth - er name for cir - cus is the Big Top?

Great big ti - ger jumps through the fire.———

Rhythm—Play these examples in G position with your right hand. | DID IT! |

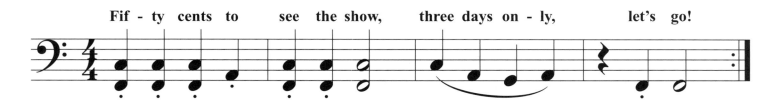

1. $\frac{4}{4}$ Don't look down, Mis-ter Tight-rope Walk-er!

2. $\frac{3}{4}$ Hors - es danc - ing, gal - lop - ing, pranc - ing.

Sight reading—Add your own fingering. Then play at a tempo you can keep steady. | DID IT! |

Fif-ty cents to see the show, three days on-ly, let's go!

I'd like to learn to ride a un-i-cy-cle some-day.

FJH2171

Rhythm—Say the words in rhythm while pointing to each note.

1. He jug - gles balls, ba - na - nas, and dolls.

2. Hear the cir - cus band, the best band in the land.

 Sight reading—Say the letter name of the notes. Then play it while counting. It's harder to say letter names then to say the intervals! That's because humans learn how to read by seeing patterns in the music. You probably read well by now, because your teacher has taught you to read by intervals/patterns. Congratulations!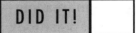

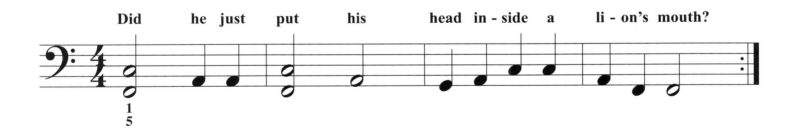

Did he just put his head in - side a li - on's mouth?

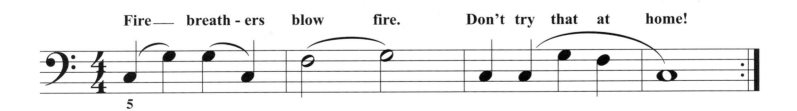

Fire— breath - ers blow fire. Don't try that at home!

Rhythm—Step in rhythm (♩ = 1 step) as you speak the words.

1.

I   would   like   to   ride   an   el - e - phant.

2. Cir - cus   ma - gi - cian,   tell   me   your   se - crets.

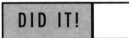 Sight reading—Follow the music by moving your eyes from left to right, and don't look at your hands.

How do they train those dogs   to walk on two legs?

I bought some pea - nuts to feed the el - e - phants.

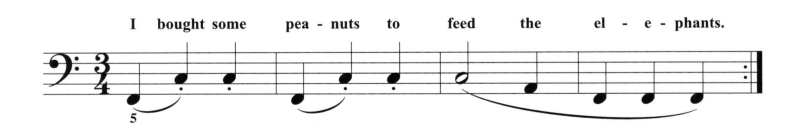

FJH217

Rhythm—Clap or count aloud, the first time **_mp_**, the second time, **_mf_**.
Then speak the words aloud while tapping.

DID IT! ☐

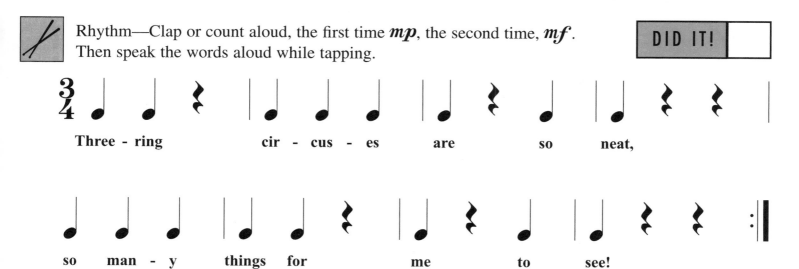

Three - ring   cir - cus - es   are   so   neat,

so   man - y   things   for   me   to   see!

ENSEMBLE PIECE Duet—Silently play the music on the top of the keys. When playing, if you make a mistake, keep going!

Fifteen Circus Clowns

Student part

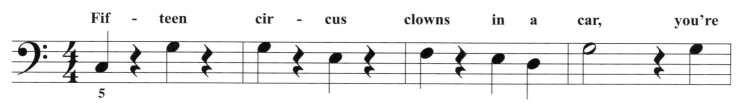

Fif - teen   cir - cus   clowns   in   a   car,   you're

packed   so   tight   that   you   won't   get   far.

Teacher accompaniment (student plays as written)

R.H. legato

? After playing, ask yourself, "Did I play with confidence?"

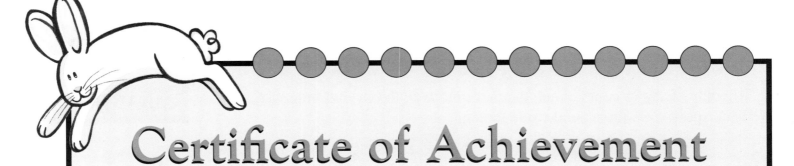

Certificate of Achievement

_____

has successfully completed

SIGHT READING &
RHYTHM EVERY DAY®

BOOK B
LET'S GET STARTED!

of The FJH Pianist's Curriculum®

You are now ready for **Book 1A**

_____

Date

_____

Teacher's Signature